60 SECONDS TO
"WOW!"

SCOTT H. LEWIS

60 SECONDS TO
"WOW!"

*Easy to Master Skills that Move Your
Audience and Build Your Career*

RALPH, HARLAND & CO.
PUBLISHERS

60 SECONDS TO "WOW!"
Easy to Master Skills that Move Your Audience and Build Your Career

Copyright ©2012 Scott H. Lewis

ISBN-13: 978-1481839242
ISBN-10: 1481839241
LCCN: 2012924149

Chapter illustrations by Michael McPhee, Laughtercraft
(http://tinyurl.com/bqjzryt)

Contact: Editorial@Ralph-Harland.com

*For everyone engaged in the lifelong pursuit of learning,
of self-improvement, and of excellence;
and for the mentors, coaches and colleagues
who provide them with support and encouragement
along the way.*

Contents

INTRODUCTION

These quick little essays on aspects of the art of effective public speaking and the craft of making presentations that engage audiences are derived from a series of weekly tips I created in 2012 for clients and friends. Every week (more or less), a different short essay was dispatched to everyone on our mailing list. We called these '60-Second Seminars' because they were brief, straight-to-the-point tips that readers could put to use that very day, if they desired.

Sending regular e-mail messages can be a bit nerve-wracking. How may are read? How many are routed to the abyss of the 'spam' file? How many are utilized? Do the readers agree or disagree?

I thrive on feedback and immediate gratification, so it was tough to send out these '60 Second Seminars' each week and not see or hear recipients' reactions. It was only after people mentioned them to me – in person or via e-mail – that I received the feedback I wanted.

And the response was gratifying: For every irascible soul on our list of contacts who demanded that we stop sending our weekly tip, there were tens of others who forwarded the e-mail to every colleague. Some recipients say that they kept the tips for future reference. Others posted and re-posted these little seminars on Facebook. We're pleased that readers see value in them and have shared them with friends and colleagues all over the world.

Several recipients mentioned that they had saved the weekly tip in a file on their computer for future reference, and that lead to the idea of gathering the tips together ourselves. A short quick-reference book seemed a worthy effort, and one that speakers could refer to and use.

The book market doesn't need another long, involved treatise on public speaking or creating effective presentations. Reading those books can be a worthwhile and enjoyable use of your time, but not if you have a presentation this afternoon. That's when this book will be useful.

The value of "60 Seconds to 'Wow!'" is in its brevity. If you read the best books on the art of making a great presentation, and jotted down the key points from each of them, you would very likely have something like this book. Herein, you'll find short, no-nonsense pointers that you can put into practice today.

It's like getting a quick coaching session delivered before you begin working on your next big presentation, with a refresher as you get ready to deliver it. This handbook is an information degustation; a buffet of ideas. Incorporate as much of the advice as you can, when it is relevant, and leave the rest.

Over time, these new skills will become second nature to you. You'll find that you're not only comfortable giving presentations; you will even look for opportunities to stand up, become the center of attention, and speak.

At some point, you'll look back and wonder how you ever could have thought of speaking as scary, intimidating, or risky.

Education is a never-ending cycle. There are always areas we seek to improve, or new skills to acquire. The truly great speakers practice and review until every movement, inflection and sentence is automatic. How can great leaders and top CEOs spend so much time and effort on practice? They make the time, because they realize the impact they can have on people, on loyalty, and on sales in today's media-savvy environment.

They also hire mentors, coaches, and writers to help them. It's not a sign of a mammoth ego to want to be an incredible speaker. It's good business, and it pays remarkable dividends.

Giving a speech is easy: Read it from a prepared text, and you've 'delivered' it.

We aim to do more. We aspire to leave our audiences saying, "Wow!" We want your listeners to ask themselves, "I wish I could do that!"

We desire to impress and awe. The keys to doing that are in these pages.

When you're ready for more personalized assistance than is possible for a book to deliver, we are here to help. Just call or send an e-mail.

It would my pleasure to be of service!

Scott H. Lewis
Kyiv, Ukraine

SLewis@Signature-CIS.com

Chapter 1

FEAR, ITSELF

For many people, being asked to stand up and make a toast, give a speech, or deliver a presentation is an invitation for emotions to run wild: Sweaty palms are just the beginning as breathing quickens, the heart races and panic sets in.

From time to time a list makes the rounds ranking public speaking as one of the most feared activities, rating with cancer and death.

It may not be speaking that people fear at all, but rather the consequence of speaking poorly. A number of perfectly rational, non-phobic fears can be linked to public speaking. One list I found - by no means either scientific or authoritative - seems a fair reflection of the non-phobic fears most of us share. How does it fit with your perception?

TOP TEN FEARS

1. Failure
2. Death
3. Rejection
4. Ridicule
5. Loneliness
6. Misery
7. Disappointment
8. Pain
9. The Unknown
10. Loss of Freedom

Think about it: It is not the toast, the speech or the presentation that scares us, but rather the unintended consequences of the speech that we fear. Perform poorly and risk the rejection and ridicule of your audience, and failure in the eyes of your colleagues, which leads to your own disappointment and misery.

That's not a desirable outcome.

American President Franklin D. Roosevelt told his countrymen in 1933: "[L]et me assert my firm belief that the only thing we have to fear is...fear itself — nameless, unreasoning, unjustified terror which paralyzes needed efforts to convert retreat into advance."

Defeating that "nameless, unreasoning, unjustified terror" is a matter of identifying, confronting, understanding, and conquering the underlying fears. Most fear evaporates in the presence of a presentation that is adequately prepared, solidly organized, and given plenty of practice.

Some anxiety is not only normal - but can even give the presentation more of an edge, and keeps the adrenalin pumping.

Overcoming paralyzing fear is simply a matter of being prepared - of knowing your material completely. The more often you challenge yourself, the less nervous you'll be and the better you will become.

Finally, don't look at a presentation as a mountain to climb. Rather, visualize how good you'll feel when you succeed.

Chapter 2

CONFIDENCE IS KEY

If there is any one recurring theme in our public speaking training, it is the value of practice. If your presentation isn't organized well, practice will help you see its shortcomings. If your speech is too long, too short, too detailed or too basic, trust the power of repetition to point out those flaws to you. If your vocal timbre, volume or intonation isn't adequate, practice will lead you to identify those issues as well.

The adage that "practice makes perfect" is misleading. It should be "practice highlights flaws, which, once addressed, moves you closer to perfection."

Not all practice is the same, either. The best practice is captured on video so that you can review it, find the problems, and repair them. Watch your performance and be constructively self-critical. Note areas where you need to improve, but also congratulate yourself on what you do well.

Positive reinforcement is part of the practice experience, too.

Video cameras have never been more accessible than they are today. Even your phone's camera will work – this is practice! Production values aren't important.

Rehearse for an hour or so, and then take a break. Too much repetition, or practicing until you're exhausted, won't deliver the desired benefits.

Confidence flows from the knowledge that you know your subject better than anyone else and that you can present your messages with clarity and impact.

Confidence is the most valuable benefit of practice.

Chapter 3

IT'S ALL ABOUT MESSAGES

Every day, we're surrounded by messages: Short and to the point, they tell us what advertisers want the public to know. They're easy to read and to remember, but they can take real effort to write!

What are your messages? What do you want potential customers to know about your firm?

Try it: Write down up to three messages directed at one of your audiences: consumers, regulators, stakeholders, employees or any other group with which you wish to communicate. Keep each message short and to the point – just a single easy-to-remember sentence. Consider:

- "ABC Freight delivers any shipment anywhere in 20 hours or less."
- "Abernathy School graduates score in the 90th percentile on university entrance exams."
- "Chaika Airlines offers nonstop flights to every European capital city, every day."

Be specific. Avoid ambiguous terms like 'leader' and 'unique.' Create a message or messages for each of your constituencies. Then – use them in media interviews, speeches, business conversations, and sales literature. Knowing and using relevant, consistent messages helps create clearer, more effective communication.

Chapter 4

WHAT'S IN IT FOR ME?

Most speakers miss the point of speaking – in fact, most don't even come close. These ineffective speakers stand before an audience and begin their presentations by talking about who THEY are. They tell THEIR story, and they brag a bit about THEIR companies.

Ask yourself the question that your listener is asking: "Why should I care? What's in it for me?" Instead of telling people why they should listen to you, tell them how your proposal will make their lives more fulfilling and more prosperous. An audience-centered presentation will effectively get and hold peoples' attention.

"What's in it for me?" It's an important question. Answer it as soon as you stand up to speak. Then do it again and again and again throughout your presentation. Never stop reminding listeners about why they should care as passionately about your message as you do.

Presentations aren't about telling people what you want them to know, or even about telling them what you think they want to hear. Convince listeners to really care about your topic, and they'll willingly follow where you lead.

Chapter 5

OVER-PACKING

We live in a world that is stuck in "fast forward" mode. Ideas, meetings, events, projects – sometimes even jobs and relationships – whiz through our lives. Life is a blur of adrenaline and emotion as we strive to prepare for the next task without ever stopping to analyze, much less enjoy, that which we just completed.

Our hectic pace is reflected in everything we do. Asked to prepare a five-minute presentation, we cram it with 15 minutes of 'essential' information. The result is a volcanic eruption of information: Slides overflowing with text and populated by multiple charts and graphs. It leaves the listener overwhelmed and ultimately uncomprehending.

Slow. Down.

Take a deep breath.

Relax.

That monthly financial report can involve dozens of slides containing complex graphs and tables, drilled down into the last detail, or it can be as elegantly simple as the three-word phrase, "We made money."

Start with the highlights, then add information in layers until you've used most of your allotted time. Then, add a quick summation and sit down. It's an elegantly simple approach to a complex, sometimes overwhelming task.

And best of all, it works.

Chapter 6

STAND UP

One of the surest ways to capture the attention of an audience – whether it's a small group of colleagues or a hall full of potential customers – is to simply stand up. A person who stands when all others are seated instantly commands attention.

I'm amazed at how few people actually do this one simple act – something that can make them many times more effective. Instead, they squander the opportunity by remaining seated, just an anonymous 'face in the crowd.'

Why?

Many are self-conscious and don't want all those eyes focused on them. Some feel that it's somehow presumptuous. Others just say that it feels odd to stand when other speakers don't stand.

These arguments aren't persuasive. The fact is that by standing we're sending a power signal. We're saying, "Pay attention. This is important." It's a lesson we learned on the first day of school, when our teacher stood in front of the class.

Subconsciously, we ascribe attributes to a speaker who stands while we sit and listen: Leader. Power. Importance.

You may be thinking that standing to give a presentation is one way to exert control. You'd be correct. And isn't 'control' one advantage you'd like to have in business?

Chapter 7

POWER POINTLESS

Sometimes, we misunderstand the nature of 'value.' Speakers who feel that creating PowerPoint slides jam-packed with text, charts and animated graphics add value to their presentation are missing the point. Your audience wants to hear YOU – not read slides or follow the red dot of a laser pointer around a screen in a darkened conference room.

Anything you place on a PowerPoint slide is liable to distract your audience from listening to what you have to say. If you absolutely, positively must use charts, graphs or spreadsheet data, use handouts – and distribute them only after you've concluded your talk.

People who ask to evaluate our seminars often ask us to "send a copy of the slides." They don't learn much, because the slides contain visual cues, but not a lot of text. PowerPoint minimalism is a significant trend: The world's most intriguing speakers are moving away from using slides entirely. The talks presented on TED.com are great illustrations of the effective, but minimal, use of slides.

Where the eyes go, ears and minds follow. PowerPoint slides should support you. You - and not your slides – are the star of your presentation, so keep your audience's attention squarely on you, where it belongs.

Chapter 8

THE EYES HAVE IT

One absolutely guaranteed way to ensure that your audience gives you its full attention – and for you to keep that attention throughout your presentation – is to keep moving. From the time you stand to begin until you sit down (to thunderous applause, of course), use your hands, head, and feet to generate continuous action.

The eye is attracted to motion. It's instinctive. A speaker who keeps moving, scanning the crowd visually, using effective and meaningful hand gestures and walking back and forth across an imaginary 'stage' gives the audience a 'moving target' to focus upon. Since the eye and mind are inextricably connected, your message is heard and understood with greater clarity when the audience is visually engaged.

Speakers who sit behind desks or stand behind lecterns and move only their lips are doomed. They are tossing valuable ideas into the void toward an audience that is thinking of other things. If the purpose of speaking is to communicate, why not use every weapon in your arsenal?

Chapter 9

THE PUGILIST

To become an effective presenter, take a tip from professional boxers and keep your hands up and at the ready!

One worry that new speakers have concerns what to do with their hands. After all the other preparations are complete, a presenter will stand up, face his audience, look at his or her hands and have no idea what to do with them. It's almost as though these alien arms just sprouted overnight!

Here's what not to do:

- Don't grip the lectern (if there is one) and hide behind it. Exposing yourself to your audience communicates confidence.
- Don't put your hands in your pockets. This is especially true if you carry keys or coins. The jingling they cause distracts from your presentation.

- Don't clasp them in front of you (as though praying) or behind you (as a soldier at 'parade rest').

The best advice for beginners is merely to let your arms hang loosely at your sides. As you proceed with your talk and become less nervous, they'll naturally rise and gesticulate as they would in any conversation.

Professionals realize that the hands are an important tool in the presentation skills arsenal. Start with them raised, elbow bent naturally. Hands should occupy the territory between your chin and navel. They may occasionally be held higher for emphasis, but should never block your face.

Use your hands – and your entire body - to give added power to your presentation, to aid description, and to demonstrate both motion and emotion.

The human eye is attracted to movement. A speaker who moves and uses his or her body to add expression will find it much easier to capture and hold an audience's attention.

Chapter 10

PAINT MY PORCH

Here's an old joke that highlights the unforeseen consequences of not delivering instructions clearly and specifically:

An unemployed fellow knocks on a man's door one Saturday morning and asks whether the homeowner has any work for him. "I can paint, I can fix things - whatever you need done," the fellow says. "I have to earn money for my family."

The homeowner thinks a bit, and tells the fellow that he'll pay the man $25 to paint his porch. He points to his garage: "Everything you need is in there," he says.

An hour later, the fellow knocks on the door again. "I painted your Porsche," he says. "Should I paint the Mercedes, too?"

When we don't deliver messages clearly, and don't ask for feedback to ensure that the listener really understands our request, we flirt with disaster. A seemingly simple assignment ("Paint my porch") can have unintended - and unhappy - consequences.

It's perfectly OK for a speaker to ask, "Are you with me?" occasionally, especially if audience members exhibit signs of restlessness or boredom.

It's vital to adjust your presentation to the audience. If your listeners aren't well-educated or if English isn't their mother tongue, using big words or complicated concepts probably won't work well. The same goes for professional buzzwords and acronyms. Remember, the goal is to communicate effectively, not to impress your audience with your incredible intellect.

The entire communications process needs to be covered thoroughly: Send your message, ensure that it is received, confirm that the recipient understands it fully, clarify as needed, and obtain confirmation of all specifics, including deadlines.

This process is especially important in situations where there are intervening interruptions, distractions or social, cultural or language differences.

Chapter 11

THE MAN IN THE MIRROR

What's your speaking style? Or, more accurately, what would you like your speaking style to be?

Few people are born to be great orators, with a powerful presence and persuasive words to match. Great speakers are created. When great political and religious leaders, actors, businessmen and others speak, we're hearing the result of hours of experimentation and practice. Like most things, the ability to captivate an audience seldom comes naturally. It's a learned skill.

The technique is called 'mirroring' or 'patterning,' and it works like this: When you watch a speaker you admire, tune out the words. Focus only on the vocal pacing and inflections, the facial expressions, and the gestures. Emulate them.

(This works best when you're alone, by the way. A casual observer may think that you've lost your mind!)

Patterning works, but works slowly. Do it often enough – even in your mind – and you'll fall into character and become adept at this bit of mimicry. The fun part is next: Pattern on several different models, not just one. After all, you don't want anyone to say, "He's trying to sound like…" What emerges is a hybrid of the styles you've patterned, and that – with some modifications of your own – becomes your own distinctive speaking style.

Chapter 12

SEND IN THE CLOWNS

I have never heard my mother, now age 84, tell a joke. When something strikes her as funny, she laughs, of course, but telling jokes is just not part of her nature. If she were forced to tell a joke or to make a humorous remark in front of an audience, I shudder to think of what would result. It would be a disaster, certainly, and it's never fun to watch a speaker try to amuse and fail.

On the other hand, there are people who are naturally funny. These folks can toss off lines one after another. They instinctively see opportunities to use humor, they seize them, and they tie the humor to their presentation.

Speakers used to be taught to begin presentations either with a relevant quote from a famous person or with an amusing anecdote. The experts held that jokes and quotes helped 'warm up' the audience, making the listeners more attentive and receptive. In reality, they were trying to provide nervous speakers with a device that would get them over their nervousness. Sometimes it worked, but this way to open a speech has become timeworn and dull. Plus, telling a joke that goes badly does nothing to reassure a nervous speaker.

Much humor is based on making someone or some group of people look stupid or foolish. Take care to ensure that what's meant to get laughs doesn't bring offense, instead.

Using humor effectively in a presentation is difficult. It's an art best left to comedians – and even they fail to deliver on occasion. Use humor only if it meets these four criteria: The anecdote is truly funny; it doesn't offend; you deliver it well; and it is relevant to your topic.

Chapter 13

THE POWER OF THREE

Look at any newsstand and you'll see that people love lists. Magazine covers trumpet stories like: "Ten Secrets to Being Lucky," "25 Ways to Train Your Goldfish," and "104 Reasons We Love Weekends." We love lists because they claim to make life simpler, more manageable, and more clearly defined.

Long lists are fine for magazine articles. They can kill a presentation, though.

The reason: Reading and listening are different. They use different parts of the brain, and affect our attention span and memory in different ways as well. When we read, we scan, skip and focus on the areas we find most interesting. We can skip items one through four in "25 Ways to Train Your Goldfish," because we've tried them and failed. That lets us scan the list and focus on items seven and 14, which seem intriguing and potentially useful. We cannot scan a speech. We're forced to absorb information at the speaker's pace.

Speakers are well advised to keep the list to no more than three items. Our minds can retain three ideas much more easily than ten or 25 or 104. Keeping the ideas or options to a minimum also makes it possible to discuss each in detail – an option seldom open when you have dozens of points. Given short attention spans, three is the perfect number: Speaker and listener alike can remember three messages, ideas or instructions. More than that is a stretch.

Chapter 14

DEAD AS A DODO

"At the end of the day, the bottom line is that, frankly, our B2B business is as dead as a dodo!"

The bad news contained in this line, delivered during a quarterly sales meeting, isn't its only problem: The line consists of a string of clichés:

- At the end of the day
- The bottom line
- Dead as a dodo

"Frankly" may not be a cliché, but it has its own disability. It's supposed to signal that the words which follow are going to be the truth. That may be, but then what do we make of the rest of the speech? Lies?

Lazy and inattentive speakers and writers are often charged with the use, misuse and over-use of clichés. They can be seductive, after all: They come to mind easily and their meaning is universally known. Yet liberally salting a presentation with someone else's worn-out lines cheats the listener, who deserves better.

When in doubt, leave the cliché out and just use plain, unambiguous language. No business person ever irked an audience for speaking plainly. A more adventurous speaker might try painting a few word pictures relevant to the speech and industry and incorporating them into the presentation. Don't be too exuberant, though: Too many colorful allusions can ruin a presentation, too.

Chapter 15

ONE O'CLOCK SLUMP

We'd just come back into the meeting room after lunch. The room was warm and the seats were reasonably comfortable. As the first speaker of the afternoon was introduced and his Power Point slide lit the screen, the room lights were turned down low. The speaker, a big guy with a soft, deep voice, began his presentation, and soon his voice became a monotonous drone.

My mind wandered and my eyelids fluttered. I wasn't the only person struggling to stay awake.

It's called the "One O'clock Slump,' and conference planners have learned from hard experience not to start an afternoon session with a darkened room. If you're awarded the post-meal slot, either refuse it or prepare an active program – one without slides and with full audience participation. Have your group stand up, move around, ask questions, complete questionnaires, make a list, or reprioritize issues, goals or objectives. Do anything you wish, but make it active!

This is a great time to bring in a motivational speaker or to engage in team-building exercises.

If you're stuck with the time slot and have information to deliver, don't give a standard "I speak, you listen' presentation. Ask questions. Walk among the participants and question people at random. If you keep moving around the room and asking questions, you'll have captured your audience's attention and defeated the One O'clock Slump.

Surprisingly, if you get your group past that first hour after lunch, they won't succumb when the next speaker starts droning in the dark. They'll have been revived, and awake for the remainder of the day.

Chapter 16

F.A.Q.

"Thank you for your attention this morning," the speaker said. "I'd be happy to answer questions, if there are any."

The audience had lots of questions. For the next 15 minutes, the speaker answered one query after another. When she left the room, I asked her how she thought her presentation had gone.

"I think it went great!" she enthused. "They were interested and had lots of questions."

It's true that a fusillade of questions lobbed at a speaker may mean that the audience is interested and hungry for more. Most likely, though, it means that, while the subject resonated with them, the speaker gave too few details, or failed to organize them properly.

We often tell speakers to ask themselves the question that listeners ask: "What's in it for me?" Equally important to preparing a highly effective presentation is to look at your outline critically, put yourself in your audience's place, and try to determine what questions they are likely to ask.

Then answer them – briefly - in the body of your presentation.

Answering those 'frequently asked questions' won't eliminate all the questions from every presentation you give, but it will truncate any Q & A time you may be allotted. With fewer questions on their minds, listeners leave feeling intellectually satisfied. That's the ultimate reflection that you've just made a great presentation.

Chapter 17

YOUR CALL TO ACTION

Earlier, we discussed the fact that most speakers miss the point of speaking because they don't address the listener's top question: "What's in it for me?" If you don't tell your audience why they should care about your message, they'll never follow where you want to lead them.

Therein is many speakers' second-biggest problem: They don't have a distinct and undeniable call to action. Once you tell an audience why they should share your passion, you need to tell them what to do with it.

A call to action needs to be simple and direct. You aren't handing your audience a 30-page menu and saying, "Order what you like" (They'll be thinking for hours, and while they're frozen by indecision, they're asking themselves why they're even hungry!). Instead, tell them: "Order the pea soup – it's fantastic!"

What do you want your listeners to do with the information you've delivered? Once you know what action you want them to take, make it clear how to do it.

Television infomercials are famous for repeated phrases like, "Call now!" As professionals, we can be a tad more elegant about it, but the old TV pitchmen had the right idea: Pick up that phone, and call...right...now!

Failing to include a call to action is the equivalent of making a suspense movie that omits the thrilling conclusion. You've involved your listeners, you have made them care. Take the final step and give them explicit direction as to how to proceed.

Chapter 18

TO CARNEGIE HALL!

There's an old joke – it probably originated in the American vaudeville era – that says everything about our quest to improve ourselves as speakers and presenters.

A violinist is playing on a street corner for the coins passers-by toss in his hat. A man stops and asks the old fiddler for directions.

"Excuse me, sir, but how do I get to Carnegie Hall?"

The old musician looks him in the eye and replies, "Practice, practice, practice!"

The same advice is valid when we ask, "How do I improve as a public speaker and presenter?"

Practice!

Practice leads to improvement. There's no better way to learn to deliver presentations than to repeat and refine your speech until the words become part of you. When your phrases and ideas and organizations become second nature, you'll own that presentation as surely as you own your name.

Think back to your early years of childhood. How did you learn your address, phone number, and the alphabet?

Rote memorization.

The same was true later with the Pledge of Allegiance and the multiplication tables.

Repetition held the key, right?

Today, we apply those same childhood principles to deliver seamless, powerful presentations.

Is it possible to ruin a presentation by over-practicing? Possibly, but don't worry: The odds are that won't happen.

Practicing means more than reciting the same presentation over and over, though: You cannot adequately hone skills by giving a sales report to the board four times a year.

You cannot let any chance to speak pass you by.

Give a farewell toast to a departing colleague.

Stand up and speak at a community meeting.

Join Toastmasters.

Give a guest lecture on your specialty at a university.

Get out there and speak, and do it at every opportunity!   Before you know it, you'll be building effective speeches in your head with only minutes of preparation, focusing on messages, and captivating audiences.

ABOUT THE AUTHOR

SCOTT H. LEWIS is a versatile and accomplished writer, public speaker and presenter.

Mr. Lewis is managing director for the CIS region for the European division of Signature Worldwide, a global customer service and effectiveness training consultancy, and former director of Willard Leadership Training, part of Willard Advertising and Public Relations.

He has experience in the legal, government and financial services sectors, and has worked with public relations clients in packaging, airlines, hospitality, and telecoms. His favorite activity involves training and mentoring: "These are incredibly creative and fulfilling activities," he says. "I love to help people build their skills, wither it's a team from a hotel or a single executive."

He is also a former chief editor of the *Kyiv Post* newspaper and an adjunct faculty member at Peninsula College in Washington. He is the author of numerous books and published articles under his own name and pseudonyms. A complete bibliography of his signed work is available at http://tinyurl.com/98t3drc.

An American, he's lived in Kyiv, Ukraine for more than a decade.